# Handful of Stars

## Sales Mantras for Winners

Anshuman Sharma

Copyright ©2012 Anshuman Sharma

**All Rights Reserved**

**Dedication**

To my family elders

Sushila Sharma and Mahesh Chandra Pathak

**CONTENTS**

Introduction .................................................................................. 7
Sales Mantra 1 - Right Prospecting ............................................... 9
Sales Mantra 2 - Archive it .......................................................... 12
Sales Mantra 3 – General News .................................................. 14
Sales Mantra 4 – Product Mastery ............................................. 16
Sales Mantra 5 – Existing Systems ............................................. 18
Sales Mantra 6 – Industry News ................................................ 20
Sales Mantra 7 – Understand Competition ............................... 22
Sales Mantra 8 – Customer's Industry News ............................. 25
Sales Mantra 9 – Customer Requirements ................................ 27
Sales Mantra 10 – Consultative Selling ..................................... 30
Sales Mantra 11 – Build Trust .................................................... 32
Sales Mantra 12 – Instant Rapport ............................................ 34
Sales Mantra 13 – Follow-Up ..................................................... 36
Sales Mantra 14 – Presentation Tools ....................................... 38
Sales Mantra 15 – Speak, but Optimally ................................... 40
Sales Mantra 16 – Body Language ............................................. 41
Sales Mantra 17 – Listen to Customers ..................................... 43
Sales Mantra 18 – Job Satisfaction ............................................ 45
Sales Mantra 19 – Dynamism .................................................... 46
Sales Mantra 20 – Self-Motivation ............................................ 47
Sales Mantra 21 – Utilize Support ............................................. 49

Sales Mantra 22 – Rejection ....................................................... 51

Sales Mantra 23 – Connectivity Tools ........................................... 53

Sales Mantra 24 – Time Management ......................................... 55

Sales Mantra 25 – Belief in Self ................................................... 57

Sales Mantra 26 – Productivity .................................................... 59

Sales Mantra 27 – Get Things Done ............................................ 61

Sales Mantra 28 – Belief in the Product ...................................... 63

Sales Mantra 29 – Self-Control .................................................... 65

Sales Mantra 30 – Innovation ...................................................... 67

Sales Mantra 31 – Belief in the Company ................................... 69

Sales Mantra 32 – Never Talk Bad .............................................. 71

Sales Mantra 33 – Pleasing Personality ...................................... 73

Sales Mantra 34 – Network .......................................................... 74

Sales Mantra 35 – Closing the Sale ............................................ 75

Sales Mantra 36 – Meet the Right People .................................. 77

Sales Mantra 37 – Cold Calls ...................................................... 80

Sales Mantra 38 – Avoid Push Sales ........................................... 82

Sales Mantra 39 – Get Buy-ins .................................................... 84

Sales Mantra 40 – Love for Travel ............................................... 86

Sales Mantra 41 – Dressing and Grooming ................................ 88

Sales Mantra 42 – Perseverance ................................................ 90

Sales Mantra 43 – Know When to Move Out .............................. 93

Sales Mantra 44 – Intrapreneurship ............................................ 94

Sales Mantra 45 – More Value to Customers ............................. 96

Sales Mantra 46 – Learner ...................................................... 98

Sales Mantra 47 – Feedback .................................................... 99

Sales Mantra 48 – Objections ................................................. 101

Sales Mantra 49 – Receive Payments ....................................... 103

Sales Mantra 50 – Repeat Sales ............................................... 105

Sales Mantra 51 – Self-Branding .............................................. 107

About Author ........................................................................ 109

# Introduction

An organization consists of various departments working together to produce products or deliver services to the market. The main objective of every organization is profitability and maximizing shareholders value. For every organization, the market is the playground and sales teams are the front line players. Sales people are the representatives of the organization who interacts with customers and combats competitors. Sales team identifies the potential buyers of the organization's products and services and connects with them to inform and convince them for the products and services they represent. They understand the requirements or problems of the prospects and try to solve them with their offerings. They face prospects queries, rejection and heat of competing sales teams offering similar products and services. A sales-person is a front line soldier.

Selling is a game of skills. A sales-person needs to do all right things to finally close the sale. Though sales team is supported by whole organization including teams from marketing, customer support and operations but they take the responsibility of company's revenues. The difference between a successful and unsuccessful sales-person is more related to the selling skills rather than the support he received from the company. This is also true that the product and service to be sold has to be good enough to be accepted in the market, as a faulty product or a substandard service cannot be saved even by the best sales-person of the world.

A good sales-person is committed to sales and enjoys the process of sales. She improves herself consistently to be better every day by building better relationships and closing more sales. She meets her sales targets and asks for more. She is liked and trusted by organization's customers and has high percentage of repeat sales. She has the amazing ability of understating the customer's requirements and satisfying them with required product or service. She is highly efficient and dynamic and regularly takes challenges in sales. Every sales-person can be great in sales, and the process starts the moment she decides to be better in selling.

This book would try to create great sales teams full of excellent sales-persons. This book would list the attributes of a perfect sales-person and describe ways to develop those skills. Selling can be an interesting and exciting journey for a successful person who could reach to the pinnacle of her organization. This resource would try to lift the competencies and career of every reader to a much higher level, if she follows the ideas specified and customize them in her own context.

This book is not a textbook seeking to describe the concept of selling instead it is an action book which can be immediately put to use by any person who want to excel in sales. The book is written in simple and lucid form so as to help even a layman to excel in sales.

This book can be read in any format suitable to the reader; she can start from chapter 1 or choose to read any chapter from the book. But it is necessary to read every page and understand the idea in your own context and implement it immediately. I hope to add substantial value to your sales career.

## Sales Mantra 1 - Right Prospecting

A good sales-person is great at prospecting as she wants to be clear about her focus area. Right prospecting is equivalent to firing at the right target, instead to firing anywhere, which would be the waste of time and efforts. She would put a substantial amount of time in identifying the potential buyers with higher probability of buying. Her sorting process would include putting the intelligent parameters for filtering the names of people with high probability of buying. This initial effort would save her from wasting her efforts on people with no intention of buying her products.

Prospecting is the first step of the sales process. It is the process of identifying the potential buyers of the company's products and services. This also includes collecting the contact details of these potential buyers so that they can be contacted and met. The database of potential customers can be generated on Internet or bought from the professional private or public agencies. Some companies involve in the practice of generating data themselves by creating a dedicated team for target market data collection. This database can also act as a company's edge in market for selling its products and services. The current technologies have created resources to collect huge data about the potential customers. This data can be processed to create information for better prospecting which would lead to higher conversion rates.

Wrong prospecting would increase the size of database as it would also include people with low or no probability of buying your products. Hence, without proper prospecting you would be extremely busy, but with low productivity. Your efforts would lack required efficiency and effectiveness, which may lead to demotivation. The initial time spend on sorting the database has high value proposition.

The simplest way of improving the sales productivity is to meet the right people with need for your products and services. These prospects would be more open for understanding the features of your offerings and would have a ready budget to close the sales deal. This idea leads to the formula that improved prospecting is equivalent to higher sales effectiveness.

The sales team needs to have the complete clarity about the potential customers of the products and services of the company. A proper profile sheet needs to be created about the people with higher probability of buying. Team also needs to generate the quality database of the potential customers with necessary details of each prospect. The necessary parameters of the sorting have to be decided and final list of prospects is to be generated. You can have the priority listing of prospects sorted, in decreasing order, with probability of buying.

You should develop the right system of prospecting in your company. The major points for this system include:

- Identification and collection of data for target customer segment.
- Deciding the parameters for selecting the prospect.

- Creating the prospect list with expected probability of buying, arranged in decreasing probability order.
- Keeping your sales funnel full with quality prospects.

## Sales Mantra 2 - Archive it

The winner sales-person is the master of documentation. She documents every relevant activity and interaction. This may include the following points:

- The minutes of the sales meeting
- The minutes of the client meeting
- Requirements of the client
- Complete details about client e.g. personality, likes & dislikes, decision makers, limitations etc.
- The observations about the client
- The research about the client
- Databases of prospects, competitors, support companies etc.
- Research about competing products and services in the market
- Other sales related materials which can be used for initiating and closing the sales

The habit of documenting keeps the sales-person fresh with every client details and supports her by providing personalized attention to her clients by keeping all her interactions and communication in a fine thread. Currently, many tools and software are available to aid sales team with documentation, which improves the effectiveness of sales-person drastically.

As documentation can be a monotonous and boring work, so it needs to be done selectively, only information and data which has present and future value must only be documented. Management tools can be used to improve the productivity of this effort.

The value addition of sales documentation is huge. It keeps your best customers at the top of your mind and allows you to provide personalized attention to them. It keeps you fresh for every meeting and up to date with any past interaction and communication, which helps you to build and maintain a good rapport with the client. Rapport is required for building long-term relationships with the customers.

Proper documentation would help you by giving more sales and improving profitability. This would help you by increasing your list of satisfied customers, who would like to connect and interact with your sales team. The documentation is also important to capture the database and tacit knowledge for the newly recruited sales team.

The culture of note taking is mostly top down. The top managers and leaders should encourage it by creating required systems and procedures. The team needs to be trained by internal mentors or external consultants to improve their documenting skills. The performance of the sales team should also be associated with quality of documentation and its proper usage to get success in sales.

## Sales Mantra 3 – General News

Every sales-person needs to be aware about the happenings in the world and their impact on their business and products. A sales-person who is aware about the local, national and international news is better than the one who is blank about the important events of the world. Present day customers are intelligent and knowledgeable and expect logical conversations with sales agents. The customer's decisions are also affected by the events and trends in the market, therefore the knowledge about them is important. A sales-person who is able to connect with her customers with her understanding of major factors would be more successful at selling.

You are not expected to know the in-depth analysis of every news article of local, national and international news but to have a feel of major factors impacting your sale. You also need to know about its effect on your customers. It also does not mean to know the news just for knowing, without right facts or interpretation. It is better to be ignorant than to speak any illogical stuff.

A knowledgeable sales-person would be considered as caring and concerned about the interests of the customers. She can use this knowledge to present her case about her products and services. She would be able to connect better with her prospects and would be trusted for her suggestions.

The sales team should be aware about the local, national and international news which, directly or indirectly, affects their products & services, their industry and their customers. They need to know about the facts and macro analysis of these events. Finally they need to develop the arguments for increasing their sales.

Sales team can develop their own system or they can take the help of marketing department to introduce general news analysis for sales-personnel. The executives responsible for gathering and analyzing local, national and international news would pick the right news articles and prepare the summary of these with the analysis in reference to customer, industry and products. This summary can be mailed or discussed with sales team on weekly basis.

## Sales Mantra 4 – Product Mastery

It is easy to encounter a sales-person who is not able to answer all questions related to her product or service or who would easily get confused about the features of the product. This is the event which every sales-person must avoid. This situation would break the trust between sales-person and the prospect as he would doubt her sincerity about selling her products and services. This is also an extremely embarrassing situation for sales-person, which may demoralize her. Sometimes, the questions asked by prospects are too technical to be answered by any sales-person, for these situations the sales-person must have a technical support system for aiding her with the technicalities of the solution offered. You can encounter cases where a business software sales-person knows about the features of the software but is not able to answer solutions offered by her software for the problems faced by the prospect company. In this case, the prospect is not looking at the solution to his problem, but software with some features, which is the wastage of his time. Every product and service must be explained in context of the prospects requirements. This is one of the major mistakes of sales-persons, as they keep talking about their product features, without understanding the need of the prospects. In all cases this sales deal will never close. The sales-person would face the rejection without knowing that the prospect could have been a potential customer.

The knowledge about the product and service to be sold by the sales-person is the fundamental requirement of selling. It is amazing to know that most sales-persons know only the basics of their products and services and are not able to handle complex and probing questions of decision makers. This weakness of the sales-person spoils the brand of the company selling the product and also puts a question mark on any future deal with the prospect.

The sharp and in-depth knowledge of the products and services sold by the sales-person can also be a differentiating factor for her. This knowledge impresses the prospect who can easily discuss his requirements with the sales-person. It would be the genius of the sales-person to solve the problem or fulfill the requirements of the prospect with her products and services.

Many companies lack serious ness in product training, which is one of the initial phase of selling process. Every sales-person must be trained to be an expert of the products and services which she is selling. She also needs to understand the prospect's requirements or problems and developing solutions with the company's offerings.

Design an exhaustive training program for sales team. Every sales-person must be the master of the products and services sold by the company. They also need to understand the general requirements of the prospects and have skills to diagnose the prospects problems and requirements.

## Sales Mantra 5 – Existing Systems

The sales-persons need to be aware about the existing solutions and systems used by the prospect. This is important to understand the problems and requirements of the prospect. Sales-person should try to procure this information even before meeting the prospect to develop the impactful and relevant pitch and presentation for the prospect. Sometimes, the first meeting with the prospect is used to understand the existing systems in the prospect's company and their link to the problem and the requirements of the customer. It is required that the sales presentation include the brief mention of these systems and the reasons of the fit of your products with the prospect's systems.

The purpose of this analysis is to build a better case for selling. You can use the data and information provided by the prospect to build a strong case for presenting the value proposition of your product. You can also identify the alternate solutions, which can also be presented to strengthen your case for selling. Your objective is to present to your prospect the case for ideal product for their organization.

You can pre-plan to study the existing solutions and systems used by the prospect. Learn to discuss these issues during your initial sales talks. Get all the required info. You can develop a case for your offerings with stronger value proposition and lower costs. You need to be ready to answer the questions raised in the process. You should include existing system analysis in the prospecting process and train the sales-persons for extracting the required information from the prospect.

## Sales Mantra 6 – Industry News

Sales team need to be aware about their industry news, which includes business and technical news. The broad points of the business activities in their industry and basic s of latest updates in technology would be enough for the sales agent. This news is generally available in industry related journals, newspapers and magazines. It is also important to know their link with their company, products to be sold and customers.

Customers do not expect sales people to be experts in business and technology, but they need to know about all the required information related to selling their products and services. They may not know about the latest research of their domain, but they need to know about the competing technology available in the market and the reasons of the suitability of their offering for the customer.

This knowledge proves the sincerity of the sales-person in-front of the customer. It shows that the sales-person like sales and want to learn more about their products and markets. It makes customer to feel satisfied, as all required information is provided to him for taking decisions.

This knowledge would build trust between sales-person and prospect and would build better connection between them. As prospect would buy from the person whom he trust, thereby, this knowledge would act as one of the factor for building trust. Technical and marketing teams can help sales people by keeping them updated with latest industry news. They can brief the sales team on important business and technology related aspects on fortnightly basis.

Call a meeting with the managers of operations and marketing departments. Brief them about the requirements of the sales team. You can also involve your top management in this process of creating a required system. The responsible persons would need to collect the summaries of all relevant business and technology news of industry and mail that to sales team twice in a month.

## Sales Mantra 7 – Understand Competition

For being a good sales-person, it is generally believed, that you need to have the thorough understanding of your products and services while the analyzing competition is the task of marketing team. But, the experienced sales-person would vouch for the study of the competitors and their products and services. This understanding adds a lot of value to your presentations and discussions with your prospect, as you are able to differentiate your products in the crowd of competitor's products. You should analyze and understand all competing products and services available in the market and get the complete details about each of them. You should also be able to identify the uniqueness of your offerings and reasons for their differentiation from competing products. You should have all required documents, data and information about the facts related to competitors and their products. This information would be useful at the time of convincing the prospect about your offerings. Most of the time the prospect would quote the half-baked information and data about the competing products, to negotiate with you for low prices. This pressure can be diffused with your knowledge about the market, industry, competitors and the requirements of the prospect, which would support you in building and presenting logical arguments for the superiority of your products and services. The prospect would appreciate the discussion and interaction with you and respect you for your knowledge.

This does not mean to speak wrong about your competitors and present false information about them. This attitude is self-defeating as sooner or later it would be caught by the customer, spoiling your brand and image. It should be clearly understood that the prospect, if possible, would be fooled only once. Selling your products with false information cannot be a right method of sales as it leads to very high cost of selling to one customer. You need to be moral and fair in your fight for superiority in the market.

Knowledge about your competitor is helpful in many ways. It helps you to know the standing of your product in the market and to find its strengths and weaknesses. This understanding supports you to work with operations team to improve the product with your feedback. It also helps you to understand the dynamics of the market and the various forces and parameters active in the market. All this knowledge would help you to build a strong case for your product and to convince the prospect to close the sales deal. You need to keep yourself updated with latest information to maintain this edge over competing sales-persons.

These efforts would help to become a better salesperson by meeting your sales target, even beating them. Prospects would be impressed by your honest and understanding and would prefer to have long term relation with you instead of any other sales-person. To be a winner you need to beat your competitors in sales.

You need to work with your marketing department to excel in this area. The marketing team is in constant touch with the market about the competing offerings and substitutes. They have the detailed analysis of each competitors and their products and required comparisons with your products. If your company does not have a full-fledged marketing department, then you need to do this analysis yourself. You need to identify all the companies offering competing products and services in the market. You need to analyze their offerings, customers, segments, sales processes, customer feedback and their image in the market. You should also try to get the documentary proofs for your analysis, to produce those documents e to support your case, if required.

You should work with the marketing department or independently to gain the complete knowledge about your competitors and their offerings. Identify the standing of each competitor in the market and the points which supports or oppose them. You can develop an compete folder for competitor's analysis, which can be used by the sales team.

## Sales Mantra 8 – Customer's Industry News

The sales-person needs to know about her prospect's company and industry. This information would be available in the industry specific journals and magazines. You also need to analyze the news related to your customers and their company. You can analyze the business, operations and financial data and information of your prospects to present relevant and sharp arguments while pitching for sales.

You need to have the broad understanding about the prospect's company and industry, not the minute details and technicalities, which you are not supposed to know. You should not explore the areas which are incomprehensible and complex, due to technicalities. Talking about these complex issues may leave you embarrassed in front of customers.

This is important as this information would help you to develop your sales strategy, which is developed based upon the perceived requirements of the customers and prospects. The industry news of your customer would keep you aware about the challenges and solutions existing in prospect's company. This information would also help you to build the cases for selling your products and services. You would be able to talk with the facts and information, which would help you to connect better with prospects and customers.

Customers would appreciate you for your efforts and would be more open to you with their challenges and problems.

They would describe their requirements clearly and allotted budget for it. This information is extremely important for sales-person, who can design her proposal to meet the customer requirement. This would improve the probability of closing the sales deal. The sales-person can build a relation with the customer which would evolve over time to get more repeat sales.

You need to subscribe to the news sources of your client's industry news. You should be able to link the analysis of this news to your selling process. Do this on the weekly basis.

## Sales Mantra 9 – Customer Requirements

It is difficult for a sales-person to close the sale by pushing her products and services onto the prospect without understanding his requirements. Customers are intelligent and smart and they cannot be tricked into buying an unwanted product. The right way to do is to have a clear understanding of his requirements and problems and solve them through your products. You need to make him talk about the challenges, problems or requirement of a product or service. Your task is to listen and ask right questions to get clarity about his intentions. You can even repeat your understanding of his requirement for his approval by saying something like "what I understand from your discussions that you need…". You can than analyze the fit of your offering to his requirements.

Understanding the customer requirements is a necessary skill for a sales-person. Most of the time the customers do not know their problems or are not able to explain it to the sales-person. A winner sales-person would have the ability to ask the right questions and would be able to describe the requirements in clear terms to her customer. This description needs to be so good that the customer would himself be amazed by your understanding of his requirements. This initial rapport can make you his consultant, who can produce solutions to satisfy him. This skill is generally developed with experience and extensive interactions with your customers. You need to have the required knowledge and intelligence to ask the right questions to make him clarify his needs. Your questions can be closed ended or open ended, but you need to be careful that these questions do not bother your prospect. The end of interaction should lead to a satisfactory need identification for which prospect is ready to pay. This can also be referred to as 'need creation' as you create a need for your products and services which did not exist before. This need is not implanted in the mind of prospect with your skills; rather it was present even before your meeting only that it was not clear enough to understand. For example, a sales person can create a need (not implant) for his treadmill in the mind of an unhealthy prospect, who always knew that he has to exercise to be fit.

The understanding of prospect's requirement is necessary, as without its clarity the sale will not happen, and the discussion would keep rotating in circles without hitting the right points. Requirement analysis also clarifies the credibility of the prospect, as your offerings may not be suitable for his requirements. As time is of essence in selling, therefore you need to be sure about the prospect's requirements and their potential for being your customers.

The requirement analysis would help you to build the case for selling your products to prospects. As you are clear about the requirements, you can convince them emotionally and logically. You can produce the examples and testimonials, which would have the maximum impact on the prospect. Discussions about requirements also bring you closer to your customers and build a better connection with them, which would help you move further in the sales process.

Requirement analysis starts with a vague description by customer about his requirements or your understating about their need. You need to ask the open and closed questions with focus on his requirements to get clarity. You need to practice it with your sales team and experienced sales people to get the expertise in requirement analysis.

You need to supply all the required information and data to your sales team regarding your offerings and prospects. You also need to develop a set of questions which would be used for requirement analysis. You also need to discuss various scenarios for analyzing the need. Finally, team needs to practice with each other, under the guidance of senior staff, to improve their requirement analysis.

## Sales Mantra 10 – Consultative Selling

Consultative selling is the most effective concept in selling. Here, you are not the sales-person but a consultant who has lot of knowledge about the domain, and you build a logical case to solve the problem of prospect with your products. You also tend to sell the complete solution instead of a single product or service. For this you may need to package your offering with other products to complete a solution. This is generally a strategic decision which is taken by the top management as it involves many complex branding issues. The solution selling is a concept used by business consultants who in addition to providing recommendations also supports in implementation of their recommendation, to get required output.

Consultative selling involves a lot of experience and knowledge to convince the prospect about your capabilities. You need to know more about the domain than your customer, for which you are talking. Prospect needs to trust you and your abilities to take suggestions from you to buy products. Any half-hearted or vague endeavor would fall flat, as it would be completely ineffective. Consultative selling competency comes with experience, analytical thinking and in-depth knowledge.

Consultative selling is required for $21^{st}$ century customers as they are smart and knowledgeable and ask a lot of questions. They generally do a lot of research before even meeting the first sales-person. A consultative seller has better value proposition as she is additionally adding value as a consultant, which is provided free. Some companies even perform a brief free study to build their case for selling their products.

Consultative selling builds relations. A consultative seller is a sales-person first and a consultant later. Consulting business works only on relations and competency. For consultative selling similar principle apply, your products would be sold majorly on your competencies and relationships. (In all cases it is assumed that the product offering of the seller is good, at least above average in industry).

You need to build a team of consultative sellers. As training a sales-person for consulting would be a tough job. People with consulting experience can be hired for the sales job and existing team's level is raised with training in consultative selling to utilize the principles of consulting in selling.

You could buy a small but competent consulting company, which can help you in selling your products. Alternatively, you can develop a consultative selling branch in the company, which would deal with high profile customers with an image of a consultant. A culture of consultative selling has to be built in the company.

## Sales Mantra 11 – Build Trust

Every sales-person must try to build a long term relationship with her customers, even with those prospects who could not be converted to customers. This relationship would be based upon the initial rapport developed by the sales-person, trust and value addition to the prospect. If your customers and prospects appreciate you then they would like to connect with you for long term. You need to make them your friend. It is much easier to sell to a friend than to a stranger.

Your quest for long term relationship and friendship with the customer should not be appalling for him in any way. If you force too hard or try with strange tricks then you would surely bother him, which is detrimental for any relation. You must have observed some fretting sales-persons who irritate everyone; you should not be like them.

We need satisfied customers who appreciate you and advocate for you and your products and services. They can act as references for you for approaching other prospects. If you have long term relationship with your customers then they would become your repeat customers, even calling you sometimes to order products. This relationship would also act as an obstruction for competitors to crack these customers. Few points you need to be extremely careful about are as follows:

- They should be satisfied and delighted with your products,

- Their trust on you should not be broken,
- They should get good support and attention from your company

These customers become your advocates and references. You can build case studies on them and they would testify for you.

Your team needs to be good at relationship building. Your team members should have pleasing and genuine personalities who would connect easily with prospects and customers. You can use social networking sites to connect with them. You should also use other connectivity tools to connect with them on regular basis.

## Sales Mantra 12 – Instant Rapport

A prospect judges a sales-person within first five minutes of the meeting. If she is not able to convince the prospect in this time then it is difficult to get the attention of prospect for the rest of the meeting. It is required to build the rapport with the prospect in first five minutes. These initial five minutes must develop the interest of the prospect in you, your presentation and your products and services. If you fall short of this achievement then your interaction would only irritate him, reducing any chances of selling. Every prospect is busy and talking to any sales-person is a cost to him, and he expects the value for this time. If he is not convinced with your value proposition then the interaction with you is time wastage for him, which carries a cost for him. You need to make sure that your interaction is the value for money for him.

Many sales-persons start their presentation with unrelated information, events and issues, which have no meaning for customer and he doesn't appreciate it. Some sales-persons try too hard to build rapport, but it falls down with opposite influence on the prospect. You need to be normal, brief, to the point and effective. You need to be an expert in these presentation skills with a ready initial sales pitch to build required rapport.

Initial rapport with prospect is required to take the sales discussion further, without which there will be no discussion for sales. It is said that the 'first impression is the last impression', you need to create that first impact on the prospect. It is also important to bring the prospect in the buying mode, as without it the deal will not close.

Instant rapport would build the relationship of mutual trust, respect and interest. Once you are able to build this rapport you have the liking of the prospect. The more they like you more is the probability of buying.

You should be able to read the explicit and implicit signals of the prospects, which are evident in their talks and body language. You need to have the right script to speak for creating the required impression on prospect. You can also identify various scenarios to develop a robust script. You need to have a pleasing personality and you should be able to satisfactorily answer his queries. You need to create the curiosity in prospect's mind with your presentation, which would force him to ask more questions, thereby generating more interest in your product.

Your sales team should be trained in reading the direct and indirect signals. They need to have a well-rehearsed script for initial sales pitch, which needs to be brief, precise and effective. Your team members should also endeavor to develop pleasing personalities for greater impact on prospect.

## Sales Mantra 13 – Follow-Up

You meet any successful sales-person and she would stress upon the importance of follow-ups, which is an important part of the sales process. Follow-ups are the constant interaction with the prospect after the first meeting. Most of the time the sales deal is not closed in the first meeting with the prospect, as he needs to evaluate the product and discuss the concept with his internal team. Prospect may also need time as he wants to evaluate other competing products too. Constant follow-ups are used to keep yourself informed about the prospect's decision making process and to put a slight pressure on the prospect to take decision in your favor. It is also used to get clarity about his interest in any competing product so that you could put a last ditch effort to turn the deal in your favor.

The other purpose of follow-ups is to identify gaps to be filled for closing the deal. You tend to call or meet the prospect to display your seriousness about the business and to pressurize him to speed-up his decisions. Sometimes, the prospect may be busy in some other urgent activities putting the decision on your sales deal at low priority; follow-ups can be used to raise the priority level of your deal.

You need to be careful about using follow-ups optimally and it should never be used to pressurize excessively so as to irritate the prospect. Your constant calling and meeting may create an atmosphere of unease for him, so you need to check your frequency of follow-ups frequently. Follow-ups, if used incorrectly, can add the negative value to the sales process.

Follow-ups can also be used to build your relationship with the prospect. You can identify the innovative ways to add value to your prospect in every follow-up. This value addition can be as simple as to provide additional information about the product or to greet them for some occasion.

It is important to get the clarity in the sales process to improve your productivity. It is a fact that the most of the prospects would not be your customers, so it is necessary to segregate the potential buyers from the prospect who have no intention to buy. You can differentiate them by tagging them as hot, warm and cold, with the hot tag representing the higher probability of buying and cold with no intention of buy, warm would lie in between and they have the potential to be converted to hot. You should focus on hot tagged prospects and take every possible effort to raise warm prospects to hot. Follow-up, if used correctly can improve the probability of closing the deal.

You need to design the right script for follow up and find the logical reasons and points to initiate the talk and meeting with the prospect. Sales-people have some hesitation for follow-ups as they are afraid to spoil the existing relationship with prospect. Some may have other reason to avoid follow-ups hoping that they would get a call back from the prospect. You need to work with the sales team to take out this hesitation. Also you need to be innovative in creating various ideas and tricks to initiate follow-ups. The follow-up should try to achieve its objective while improving the relationship with the prospect.

## Sales Mantra 14 – Presentation Tools

During the meetings of the sales-person with the prospect she needs to use several presentation tools to present her case to the prospect. These tools can include PowerPoint presentations, documents, testimonials, demonstrations or product samples. These are the important tools for selling, which are generally used by sales people. For example, a printer sales-person may carry the specifications of the printer in paper format and also carry the printer to demonstrate the working printer to the prospect so that it could be experienced by the prospect. Software sales-person would demonstrate the software on their laptops or smartphones and may submit the physical brochure of their product. A toothpaste sales-person can also give the sample tubes of toothpaste for its experience.

Sales presentation's sole purpose is to create a positive impact on the minds on the listeners. These presentation tools are used with promotional schemes to close the deal faster. These tools and aids need to be used intelligently and optimally. The objective of these tools and aids is to create required impact, not to create unease. For example, a presentation of 45 minutes would be a hassle for the top management of the client's company or the demonstration of a product which could affect the normal functioning of their business.

Every competing company generally relies on their presentation to create the required impact for closing the sales deal. Generally, the prospect would give the equal time to every company, including your company, to present their case and value proposition. You need to utilize this presentation time, judiciously, to convince the prospect to buy your product. You can also use the time of presentation to connect with your customers. You should encourage a lot of questioning to develop their interest in your offerings. You should keep the atmosphere of presentation light with fun and laughter.

Sales team needs to work with their marketing team to develop a high quality presentation material for sales presentation. You also need to anticipate the queries, which could be raised during the presentation and need to find satisfactory answers for them.

## Sales Mantra 15 – Speak, but Optimally

As listening is an important part of communication, similarly speaking optimally and effectively is also an important part of the communication. Speaking optimally means explaining your case in minimal but effective words. It also means that you have clarity and quality in verbal communications, with the effectiveness in your voice. Entrepreneur use elevator pitch to explain their concept to investors, same way a sales-person would use the elevator pitch to explain her case to prospect. Your talks should raise the interest level of the prospect, exciting him to ask more questions about company and your products. Speaking optimally would raise the probability of closing the sales deal.

Speaking optimally doesn't mean, in any way, to lessen the impact of your talks, it only means to create either similar or better effect using fewer words. Lesser number of words also requires less processing on the part of the prospect, thus keeping him fresh to take decisions.

## Sales Mantra 16 – Body Language

A sales-person has to be a good communicator in every aspect. She needs to be a good listener, an optimal talker, with clarity of content and with right body language. One of the most important part of sales communications is the right and effective body language. Humans can instinctively note the difference between the persons with right and wrong body language. It is necessary to create a right impact on the prospect to convert him into a customer.

Body language needs to be natural and impressive. It is used to intensify your spoken words. For instance, if you are talking about the features of your product and you express it with shine in your eyes, excitement on your face and with right hands gestures then you tend to create a more impact about the features of your products. If body language is unnaturally weak or dramatic then it is instantly visible, and the communicator is considered as fake. You need to be extremely careful about the use of body language in your communications.

You can also use it to understand the emotions of your prospect. You can notice the excitement or the irritation in the prospect's body language. You need to be skilled enough to modify your content to engage the prospect. Your body language should be natural without any drama added to it. You can learn the concept of body-language to express yourself better and to understand the non-verbal communication of your prospect.

Sales team needs to be trained in the basics of body language, so they could appreciate its importance in communication. This can be used by them to express better and to understand the prospects signals.

## Sales Mantra 17 – Listen to Customers

A winner sales-person knows the difference between listening and hearing. She also understands the right timing of speaking and listening. Listening is the most important skills of a sales-person. Some people think that blabbing is a required skill for selling, but in reality it makes the sales-person repulsive. Listening makes the speaker feel revered and appreciated. He feels that the sales-person cares about him and genuinely wants to solve the problem, instead of pushing the product to him. Strangely, listening, with all these benefits is hard to be embraced by people.

Listening is not hearing and they differ in sincerity. Your listening skills need sincerity as information gathered during customer interactions would be used to understand requirements and present your case to prospects. Most of the sales-person only try to hear their customers, not listen. Generally, listening to customers helps in rapport building with prospects, understanding their requirements and getting information, which would be required to build and present your case to finally close the sale.

The connectivity required for closing the sale starts with listening. Human beings want to be listened, which is their basic psychological requirement. The sales talk would be a right combination of listening and talking optimally. You start with talking, delivering your initial pitch which builds interest and motivates the prospect to talk, then you listens to his requirements or problems which he wants to get resolved, then you suggest a solution while building your case. This would be followed by the question and answer session, finally you close the sale.

You as a sales-person needs to keep quiet and listen to your customer with interest and honesty, only interrupting occasionally to ask questions to direct the talks of the speaker. Your sales team should be trained in communicating properly with customers and prospects. Verbal communication must be the part of sales training (which includes listening as an important subject). The team needs to practice it consistently till they get expertise in the art of listening.

## Sales Mantra 18 – Job Satisfaction

A tired and depressed sales-person would get difficulty in closing any sale as none of the customer or prospect would like to interact with this sales-person. Everybody wants to interact with the person who is happy with her life and job which she is doing. A happy sales-person spreads positivity and looks excited about adding value to the prospect or customer. You must have interacted with the sales-persons who look crushed with the weight of their job and spread negativity; you do not want to buy from them.

The happiness of a human being is genuine, it is difficult to fake. If you are not happy with the sales job then you cannot look happy and enthusiastic. You need to work with your team to resolve any troubling issues or if you do not like the sale job then you need to change the work domain to the one which you like. Any working person spends one-third of her life working, which means that you need to like your work. You should not get stuck in the work which is not liked by you and unnecessarily stresses you. If you do not like sales then it would be difficult for you to perform in it, which would waste your time and effort.

You need to evaluate your team and check for the members which are not performing well. Check for the reasons, you can try to improve them through mentoring and training. Even after all efforts, if the team members who are not able to improve their performances to the acceptable levels then they need to rethink their job in sales.

## Sales Mantra 19 – Dynamism

A winner sales-person would always be dynamic and energetic. She seems to get more energy with sales and tends to energize others with her energy. She is always confident in meeting her targets and most of the time she earns her variable component of her salary, which is linked to her sales targets. She keeps studying and learning about effective selling techniques and new products and services of her company. Her network with her customers is strong and they buy company's products because of her dynamism. These are result oriented people who do not leave any task pending. You need to understand that dynamism is not over-excitement for something which can be bothering for team and customers. Dynamisms means actions with clear focus on goals while a temporary excitement does not add value to anyone.

For a successful sales-person dynamism is necessary. Sales require meeting several people every day with different attitudes and personalities. But, an energetic and dynamic person is liked and appreciated by all.

You need to plan your day for more productivity and you need to be happy with your job.

## Sales Mantra 20 – Self-Motivation

The job of selling is full of stress, if you are not strong enough mentally and physically, you could be overwhelmed by its pressures. Sales job put many forces on the sales people like targets to meet, closing the deal, demands of the customers, travelling and pressures of personal life. To deal successfully with all these forces and to be a winner, you need a lot of motivation. This motivation cannot be external as it is affected by many other uncontrollable factors, the required motivation should be internal. Self-motivation is the positivity you get from inside. Special Forces commandos are trained in the art of self-motivation as they perform in extreme circumstances. Selling is not as tough but requires similar level of self-motivation. Your personal goals should match your organizational goals to get the required determination for the job.

Self-motivation cannot be completely related to money. The motivation of money, which most of the companies use, has its limitations. For self-motivation it needs to be more than money, it has to be something bigger than herself to which she can commit. For example, selling the lifesaving cancer medication would be more than money, as it is saving lives of millions. Many sales managers find it difficult to train their team in self-motivation.

Self-motivation is the source of energy to perform in sales. If you are motivated then you would have energy to take challenges, a demotivated person would find it difficult to even connect properly with her existing customers.

Managers need to build close personal relations with their team members to understand their motivations and their psychology. The sales manager needs to work with the Human Resource team to synchronize the personal goals of each sales-person with organizational goals. During the time of stress, for any sales-person, the manager must support her team member in resolving the issue. The team members must be supported to get the small wins. With time, they would learn to motivate themselves.

## Sales Mantra 21 – Utilize Support

There are many events in the sales process where a sales-person needs to take support of other departments in your company. Some products require the in-depth technical knowledge for the presentation, which can be provided by operations team of the company. To face the complex questioning of the prospect a technical expert can also accompany the sales-person for the sales presentation. Several times marketing team add a lot of value by providing data, information and analysis about market and competitors. The sales department needs to work with other teams of the company to enhance the impact of the sales effort.

It is required to understand that the technical presentation to the prospect is only a part of the sales presentation and the technical person in no way is responsible for closing the sale. He is only offering support to the sales team. Sales-person needs to act as a coordinator to use the skills and knowledge of other professionals of her company to improve the revenues of the company.

The managerial skill of a sales-person is an important tool to get success in sales as it requires the management of resources to achieve your her targets. The sales-person needs to develop essential contacts in the company to utilize the required resources and support productively.

Sales manager needs to conduct a requirement analysis for the support required from other teams. She needs to organize the required high-level meetings to garner required support and commitments. She also needs to support her sales team by arranging any resources required by her team to perform better.

## Sales Mantra 22 – Rejection

Rejection in sales process is the biggest truth of the sales-person's life. Rejections are common, they are almost daily. In fact, most of the prospects which the sales-person meets reject their products and services. The reasons for these rejections would vary, but the most common of them would range from 'budget' to 'problems in the product' to 'high prices' to 'not required'. Rejection hurts, even the experienced sales-persons. The sales-person feels insulted or deceived by the prospect. Actually, it is none of these; the only simple message is that the prospect has not bought from the sales-person. She needs to take her learning, smile on it and move forward.

For a winner sales-person, facing the rejection is as simple as breathing. They try their best to close the deal, in case of rejection they accept it calmly, identify their mistakes, find solutions to these mistakes and move on to next prospect. They never regret for it. While a loser sales-person would do the opposite. The rejection would affect her emotionally and regret would affect her daily life. She would lose her precious time in this unnecessary pain. She needs to correct herself.

If you are not able to eradicate the fear of rejection, then it is difficult to sell, as the fear of rejection would overpower every meeting with prospect and customer. This fear spoils your ability to perform in sales. If rejection is taken as a necessary part of the job then it loses its strength and instead adds value by improving your selling skills consistently.

To eradicate the fear of rejection you need to attend a lot a sales meeting to experience a lot of rejections. You need to keep facing rejection even if it troubles you slightly. You need to focus on the learning from each rejection and make it weak with your acceptance to it.

## Sales Mantra 23 – Connectivity Tools

Repeat sales are one of the most important components of sales. This is the business from the existing customers, who are satisfied with the products and services. The other main reason for repeat sale is the connection and relationship of sales-person with her existing customers. This relationship also helps the sales-person in getting leads and references. If you are able to bond with your customer strongly then he would support you in closing the sales. You need to find ways to keep this connection and relationship with existing customers strong. You can find reasons to send greeting cards and gifts to your major customers. You can meet you r customers at regular intervals to update them about the latest industry and product news or you can find unique reasons to meet.

These interactions and meetings with customers have one specific purpose attached to it, which is to increase sales through repeat orders and references. Most of the time your customers are aware about this purpose and support you in your endeavor to get more business. It is important to note that these customers need to be satisfied with your products and services. You need to work with your support team to ensure their satisfaction.

You should consider your existing customers as part of your business network and you need to keep wishing them on their special days. You can also send them gifts on festivals and special occasions. You should also keep updating them about your company, industry and product news. You can even call them once in a while to add value to them in some way.

Your team needs to decide on a proper process of connecting with their customers. You can take the help from best practices of other companies and industries. Your process description should include specific scenarios and actions. You as a manager need to arrange the resources to build this connection with all of your existing customers. This effort of connecting with customers should also be the part of your weekly report which would specify the efforts taken for connecting with your customers and results achieved. It needs to be understood clearly that the results from these efforts would not be immediate, but would take certain time to bear fruit.

# Sales Mantra 24 – Time Management

A sales-person who can manage time efficiently would be highly productive and successful, as she would be able to achieve much more than her peers in same amount of time. It is a well-known fact that the work occupies all the time allocated to it. For example, a one hour work can easily fill the time slot of four hours, if allotted to it. That is the reason deadlines are set for tasks and work. These deadlines need to be reasonable and logical, for instance a task which takes an average of five hours to complete should not allotted three hours to it.

Deadlines make you to perform at your peak to complete the task in allotted time, by taking support from all the available resources. Setting priorities for your work would also help you to manage your time. The most important tasks should be set with highest priorities while the least important task would get the lowest priority. The importance of the task can be calculated by the potential value it would add to the organization. It is necessary to reduce the list of urgent tasks from your daily life. Urgent tasks are mostly the pending work on edge of deadlines. To have more control on your work, you need to reduce your urgent tasks.

Time management does not mean to skip important tasks or compromise on the quality of work. It is required to maintain the high quality of your output and without neglecting any important task. Time management makes you more effective and efficient by empowering you with better output every day, in comparison to others.

For better time management in sales follow these points:

- Commit to Time management in your work
- Prepare daily priority list of work
- Set deadlines
- Do not leave any task pending
- Commit to quality output
- Keep reviewing your work performance
- Keep improving the management of your time

## Sales Mantra 25 – Belief in Self

The main difference between a winner and a loser is self-belief, which is the strong sense of confidence in your abilities. This confidence can raise a person to the peak of her career. People with self-belief take challenges and has high work productivity. They are not afraid of taking initiatives which are considered risky by others. Self-belief comes with skills, competencies and previous successes in life. People, who believe in God, generally cite their faith as the source of self-belief.

Sales-persons with self-belief are amazing. They are go-getters and take risks to close risky deals. They are learners, who learns fast to fill any gap in their abilities. They develop themselves every day and motivate others to improve themselves. Self-belief helps the sales-person to break barriers for achieving goals. She is better in facing rejections and learns from those experiences.

Self-belief is an asset in selling. A person with self-belief would accept any sales target and achieve it. This person would act as role model for others and would affect the whole team positively. Her belief in self is contagious and the performance of the whole sales team rises drastically with her presence. She is easily able to win the trust of customers and they believe in her products and services.

Self-belief is associated with results, as without output self-belief has no meaning. The quality of the sales-person with self-belief is that she is able to work extremely hard to achieve her goals and targets. This ability sets her apart from others.

To build self-belief in your team, you need to work with each of your team member to get initial successes. They need to be trained frequently to build skills and competencies. A successful and supporting culture also helps in building strong sales teams.

## Sales Mantra 26 – Productivity

A productive person is an asset to the company as she delivers more quality output than her peers. She is extremely disciplined and clear about her thinking. She never leaves her work pending and squeezes the maximum output from her time.

She has developed the required skills and competencies to perform her tasks excellently. Her daily meeting schedule with prospects is highly efficient with minimal wastage of time. She uses the cheapest and fastest mode of transport to reach to client meetings and is able to finish her meetings in least amount of time, while achieving required results. Even if she has to wait for client meetings she is seen busy in completing her other tasks using technology tools.

She works at the peak performance levels and is extremely fast at completing her tasks. She is sincere in her work and enjoys it completely. She is straight-forward in her communications and never wastes her time in any irrational activities. Fast task completion does not mean to compromise with quality of the output, instead it is completed with either same or better quality. It also doesn't mean to look fast but to actually be productive in achieving results.

Sales would be better if you meet more prospects in addition to deeper connectivity with your existing customers. If you are fast and efficient then you tend to meet more prospects and customers, thereby improving the probability of closing more sales.


You need to learn the required skills like Time Management and use productivity tools to perform more tasks productively. You also need to consistently learn new ways to be more productive.

## Sales Mantra 27 – Get Things Done

Who is a doer? She is the person without any excuses who get things done. This person does not waste time or argue on irrelevant topics, instead she is highly productive and energetic. You challenge her with any task and it will get done. She is able to achieve seemingly hard targets and close tough sales. Due to her initiatives and strengths she has developed unique skills which help her to be a task master. She is a learner and failure seems to make her stronger. She is a doer and every sales department in the industry wants her in their team.

A doer is a person who takes challenging goals and regularly breaks her selling targets. With her habit of experimenting and taking initiatives she knows every detail of the market. Her experience makes her a strong connected person in the market. She takes required help from other departments of her company and guides her team for success. She celebrates her success and motivates herself and others to break previous sales records. She keeps challenging herself with new goals and targets.

A doer would never involve herself in irrelevant activities. She is clearly focused on the high value tasks and puts her full force to it. Her criterion for choosing a task is its value proposition and challenge, she is result focused. She has big dreams to excel in sales and is fully committed to it.

A doer in sale is driven by commitment to her goals. She has clear goals in her life and has associated them with the job she is doing. Her every task and success takes her towards her goals. To be a doer you need to be a good learner to keep improving yourself for better performance every single day. You are not afraid of failures instead you learn from them, they seem to make you stronger. You identify the reasons for your failure and bridge the gap to take the challenge again, till it is won. The sales manager should work with the sales team to create doers in their team. You need to analyze the strengths and weaknesses of each team member to work on their weaknesses for making them a better sales-person. You need to check their life goals and synchronize their work with their life goals.

## Sales Mantra 28 – Belief in the Product

To sell a product, you need to believe in value proposition of the product, lacking which it is difficult to sell the product. Without the belief, you would not be able to act passionately for the product and its value addition to the customer. The prospect can easily tell the difference between a genuine and fake sales-person. A genuine sales-person would believe in what is being sold and it would be evident in her body language and her communication. The right example is the presentation of past Apple CEO Steve Jobs; he used to feel proud in presenting and selling Apple products. Every sales-person needs to learn from this master of marketing and selling. You need to feel happy and proud in selling the products to your prospects. The prospects would be able to see this passion and enthusiasm in your presentation. This passion has to be genuine as you cannot make it up. Until, you feel good about your products you cannot bring that intensity in your discussions.

You need to study the product in depth. You need to experience and feel it. You need to become the master of your product. You should meet and interact with the satisfied customers using the product. You can meet the successful sales-persons selling the product to understand their ideas about the product. You should also see the manufacturing of the product and the steps it passes through to take shape. You should also meet marketing and understand their views about the product. You need to do everything which would build your belief in your product. The interest in the product would make you dig deeper and study it further, making you the master in it. These efforts would support you in creating the required impact in the product presentations with the imposing answers of the queries raised by prospects.


You as a sales-person need to build your belief in the product you sell. You need to study the product in detail and experience its usage. You should meet the satisfied customers and seek their reasons for satisfaction. You should also learn from the successful sales-persons, who are able to close the sale skillfully.

## Sales Mantra 29 – Self-Control

Negative emotions are enemies of sales. If you are short tempered then it would be difficult for you to sell your products as some prospects would make you lose your temper. Sales need a strong mind and a stronger control over negative emotions. Sales process involves meeting new and different personalities every day, all of which will not be pleasant. Sales take you in various situations, good and bad, sometimes extremely complex. You need to have endurance and control to complete the sales process successfully. Every sales-person needs to be clear about her strategy, which means she knows 'what she will do and what she will not do', which would help her to take decisions.

The most logical formula for success in sales job is to remain calm and composed, in addition to being energetic and dynamic in sales process. Most of the prospects you would meet would be good and respectful and their actions would not hurt or insult you in any way. Sometimes, you would meet irrational people who would talk illogical and may even insult you. The best way to deal with them is to object their behavior calmly and try to take discussions forward. You need to move out of the sales meeting if the prospect keeps misbehaving. In this case you need to look for other channels to restart your sales discussions again with the prospect's company.

The attitude of remaining calm and composed is good for life as it is good for sales, it would save you from unnecessary pain and conflict. You can focus your energies on constructive actions to success instead of unproductive discussions.

You can use self- control techniques and exercises to control your emotions and outbursts. It would be great if you can set the principles (rules) for yourself to do sales, which would help you to take decisions and actions during complex circumstances.

## Sales Mantra 30 – Innovation

Sales process and techniques are generally same for most of the products and services. Almost every sales-person uses the same processes for selling stuff. The difference is in the skills, planning and strategy. It is also known that a good sales-person can sell anything as she knows the psychology of customer and science of selling.

Marketing is different in the sense that the opportunities for creativity are tremendous in advertising and promotions. An innovative marketing department is extremely strong. Sales is quite a rigid process to approach prospects, present the case and close the deal. But a winner sales-person is innovative in sales process too.

Decision makers in customer's companies keep meeting a lot of sales-persons every day. Their days are full of similar presentations, demonstrations and negotiations. They keep hearing the sales pitch over and over again with fake excitement and optimism. This is quite boring for every decision maker. The creative presentations, innovative discussions and genuine charm are the breath of fresh air for the customer, which would attract the attention of the buyer.

You need to be careful not to shock the customer in any wrong way, which may spoil the relationship and the chances of sale of products and services. Your creativity and innovation must be within the acceptable limits of customer. One sales-person can be creative in presenting the product while other sales-person can be innovative in closing the deal or presenting the proposal. But they need to be pleasant and creative enough to delight the customers. The creativity would also ease the strict business atmosphere. You can also introduce some fun elements in the discussion, which would make customer associate you with pleasant experiences.

Sales team should regularly brainstorm the new ideas to attract the attention of customers and close the sales. These ideas should be tested and refined to make them presentable in-front of customers. These ideas should be practiced and rehearsed by sales-personnel to get expertise in executing. Before implementing any new idea in your sales process, you need to check your company policy for introducing any new idea in sales process.

## Sales Mantra 31 – Belief in the Company

As a sales-person your personal goals should match with your organizational goals, as that makes you work and perform at your peak. Any mismatch between these set of goals can make you unsatisfied with your job, leading to weak performance and conflicts. You will not be able to respect your company and its values.

You need to have the belief in your company. For your best performance at work you should respect your company, its policies and its mission. From the company's perspective, the top management should understand the requirement of making every employee feel positive about the company. The Human Resource Department has the responsibility of ensuring positive atmosphere in the company. This positivity would make you to put your maximum energy and efforts for company's success, which in-turn would make you successful. The concept of ESOP (employee Stock Option Plan) was based on the similar logic. A satisfied employee works hard with sincerity and feels happy about doing her job. You appreciate your company and enjoy your work. You tend to take initiatives for the success of your company. You act like an entrepreneur inside your company.

If your relation with company is only to complete the instructed tasks, then it is the waste of your potential and this relation would be lose-lose. Your job should be of your liking and interest. The sincerity and honesty for your company is also important, as it fills you with motivation.

To connect better with their employees, companies associate themselves with CSR (Corporate Social Responsibilities) activities, by adding value to society through various activities. These activities motivate employees and allow them to connect with the company and its policies better.

It is the responsibility of sales manager and Human Resource team to make the sales team believe in the company. They need to work with each of the sale personnel to improve them and support them in meeting their goals and sales targets. Their complaints and conflicts need to be resolved satisfactorily. They should be trained frequently to improve their skill-set. The company should help them to believe in themselves. The objective of the sale orientation program for new recruitment has the same purpose, to build the trust in the company. The orientation program describes the history of the company and its achievements. It talks about the value addition of the company to employee's lives and to the society. The top management need to take special care to build a culture of trust in the company and employees should believe in the goals and mission of the company.

## Sales Mantra 32 – Never Talk Bad

A good sale person would never misinform or speak critically about anyone, even her competitors. She remains extremely careful in-front of customers and description about competitors and substitutes would only remain to specification of facts. The habit of putting down your competitors, to prove them weak in front of your customers, generally back fires. Though, you can specify the facts and let them interpret and analyze that information to come to a conclusion about your competitors. But, you should never try to put your words, about the competing offerings, into their mouth. Any wrong action may damage the credibility of the sales-person.

For describing your competitors you need speak in a positive language, specifying the facts, data and information which would help the prospect to create the true interpretation about them. Definitely, you would not want to paint a great picture about your competitors by giving the information about their successes, instead you would provide information about your competitors, which would help you to close your sales. This information could be about generic features of the product not focused on the niche segment of the prospect or the weak support in the prospect's geographical area. You are like a consultant to the prospect helping them with information, which would help them to take decisions, hopefully, in your favor.

The discussions of the sales-persons should be focused on describing their own products and services and presenting the value proposition. The discussion about competitors needs to be incidental and should be limited to specifying information, in the positive way, to help them take decisions. You need to be ready with complete analysis about your competitors and their products and services.

The sales team needs to be trained to handle these types of situations. As a manager you need to give them complete information about the competitors and their offerings in the market, equipped with proofs and documents, which could be presented to prospect, if required. You also need to have the comparison chart between your offerings and competitors, proving your uniqueness and superiority. The team also needs to be trained in presenting these with positive language, without bad-mouthing your competitors.

## Sales Mantra 33 – Pleasing Personality

A sales-person with pleasing personality is liked by all, her team and her customers. Pleasing personality means that she is charming, fun loving, positive and genuine. She enjoys her work and remains enthusiastic for meeting her prospects and customers. This sales-person fills the sales meeting with life by keeping the atmosphere of meeting light with laughs and smiles, without diluting the seriousness of the business meeting. She connects easily with prospect and customers and has ease in closing her sales deal.

People want to connect with pleasing personalities. They want to do business with them, which makes these sale people more successful. Pleasing personality has to be natural, you cannot fake it. You need to be happy and satisfied with work and in life, to have a pleasing personality. Your attitude also defines the way you live your life, which needs to positive and supporting. A sales-person should try to improve her personality and image to become more approachable and likable.

The sales manager should also build her team with pleasing and attractive people. She needs to hire professionals with pleasing personalities, as it is difficult to change them afterwards. Regular training should be provided to the sales team to communicate better with customers.

## Sales Mantra 34 – Network

The speed of your sale depends upon the size and depth of your network. It is a general formula which links the size of the network with experience of the sales-person. The network of a sales-person generally consists of professionals from industry and customers. The people in the network have good connections and support each other for getting success. The network of sales professional helps them with leads in the market to pitch for sales, which means it connect you with ready buyers. It also helps you with references and testimonials of customers and consumers of your products and services.

The value of these networks is so strong that some experienced sales professional get most of their sales through these networks and customer relations. Some of these sales professionals have such a good name in the industry that they are considered as an expert or a celebrity. The members of these associations and networks add value to each other in various ways and personal relations evolve between like-minded people. These relations would be extremely useful in future for your work.

You can join your industry and customer's business associations. These associations keep conducting events, programs and meetings which help you to expand your network. You can also use the social networking platforms to connect with your customers and prospects. You can support them with your suggestions, guidance and new information about your products and services.

## Sales Mantra 35 – Closing the Sale

Closing the sales is the most important part of the sales process. Its importance is evident from the fact that closing the sale is the objective for which the sales process is initiated. Closing the sale means to get into the deal with prospect to sell your products and services. Sales close transform the prospect into a customer. This also means that the prices, payment schedule and quantities to be purchased are decided and major terms and conditions are finalized. This is the point of success for sales-person. Some companies consider the closing as the second-last step in the sales process, while the last step is the final payment collection from the customer. The last step is important as some customers create problems in making payments. In most companies it is the responsibility of the sales-person to collect the payment from the customer. Collection of complete payments by sales-person is the only criteria for achieving the target for these companies.

The verbal commitment of the prospect would not be considered as closing; instead it must be in black and white i.e. agreement agreed and signed on paper (or digitally). The weakness of the verbal commitment is evident from the fact that it can be misinterpreted and modified with strange logic and interesting reasons. The deal agreed and signed in black and white has credibility and has consequences for both buyers and sellers, if the agreed terms are not met. Close of sale is accompanied with certain terms and conditions which are applicable to both buyers and sellers.

Every sales-person must concentrate on the close as without this focus she would move in circles, with no end in sight, which would be the waste of time and resources for the organization. The sales-person needs to pull every sales process towards close. The prospects and customers need to know about the purpose of the sales-person is to close the sales for which they are interacting. The sales-person needs to be straightforward in asking the prospect for closing the deal as almost every prospect needs to be pushed for the close. The sales-person needs to move on if prospect has no intention of closing the sales deal.

The sales manager needs to stress upon the importance of close to every team member. It should be considered as the most important part of the sales process, in addition to building the satisfactory relationships with customers. Team members should also be trained in the art of effective closing without wasting time and effort.

## Sales Mantra 36 – Meet the Right People

The decision making authority to buy products and services lies with limited executives of the prospect's company. It is important for the sales-person to meet the right people who have decision making authority. Most of the time it would be difficult to meet these decision makers as every sales-person would like to meet them, so these executives put a layer of people and managers between them and sales-persons. They can be called 'insulators' as they block your messages to reach to the right people. The objective of insulators is to filter the sales-persons and let the right people pass through. But, most of the time this layer wastes a lot of time and resources of the sales-persons. The best option for the sales-person is to meet the decision maker directly, who would either take the decision to buy or would refuse to buy, clearing you to move forward.

A sales-person encounters a major problem when she encounters layers of insulators which resist her to meet the decision makers. If the executives of insulator are sincere people who are serious about supporting the decision maker, then a good product & service with nice presentation would convince them to pass you through to the right people. If the sales-person is smart then she can convert these people as advocates of her products. Many times, these insulators are present there to block you from reaching the decision makers and waste your time and resources. You need to cross them with your capabilities or choose another channel to reach the decision makers. A sales-person must be good at differentiating between decision makers and insulators.

The best option would be to prospect right at the initial stage of the sales process. Professional databases are available in the market with contact details of the right managers and decision makers. Sales-person can use these databases to connect with the right decision makers.

One of the good strategy is the 'top down approach', though it cannot be applied in every situation, but it should be used frequently. There are two types of strategies for approaching the prospect, 'bottom up' and 'top down'. 'Bottom up' strategy means the sales-person starts from the reception of the company or the front end executive and move through the insulators to reach the decision maker. 'Top down' strategy means that you start at the top and that top executive refers you down in the hierarchy for presentation and demonstration. For example, to sell a technology product, if you interact with the COO (Chief Operating Officer) of the company and then she refers you to the technology head of the company who would take decision for buying the product. This reference has credibility as it is coming from the top and your presentation would have sincere audience.

'Top down' approach is much impactful and faster than 'Bottom up', but in many situations the only option is approaching through front end executive. A sales-person needs to develop the skills to cut through the insulators to reach the right decision maker.

You should get the profession databases, which are updated frequently, that would help you to contact the decision makers, thereby reducing the sales cycle time. You also need to understand that meeting the decision maker is full of risks as any mistake during presentation would be fatal and you may not get the second chance in the company.

## Sales Mantra 37 – Cold Calls

Cold calling is one of the important aspect of selling and many sales-persons use it to meet the potential buyers. This is a type of prospecting where the sales-person call or meet the prospect unannounced and without any appointment. The sales-person makes unsolicited calls to the target segment even without knowing that they are prospect or not. The percentage of success in cold calls is extremely low and may leave a bad impression on potential customers. The logic of cold call is the chance that the meeting or call is made at the right time when the person is looking for the similar product like yours and is free for meeting and discussions. Most of the time the responsibility of cold call is either outsourced or the younger sales staff takes the lead. The decision of the cold calls is taken based upon the successful previous experiences and ROI.

Prospecting by cold calling has low productivity as most of the efforts and resources go waste, without any returns. The better way is the systematic prospecting using a proper prospect's database and prefixing the sales meetings for discussions and demonstrations. The planned sales process is many times more effective than cold calls.

Some commodities items are sold mostly by cold calls. For example, office stationary is sometimes sold through cold calls. Office stationary is required by almost all organizations and the pricing and quality differences between products are minimal. These commodities products are majorly sold on price difference. In this case the sales manager would flood the market with sales agents with good pricing and ready to sell products.

You need to check the suitability of the cold calls in your sales process, which should have high ROI. Based upon your analysis a part of prospecting can be done with cold calling.

## Sales Mantra 38 – Avoid Push Sales

Ask someone to visualize a sales-person and it is a high probability that they will visualize a person trying hard to sell her products, even irritating the potential buyer. This type of sale is generally considered as push sales, where a sales-person relies on her ability to pressurize the buyer for buying the product. Push sales is the concept used by sales-persons who are just concerned about selling their products, without any concern for the buyers requirements and emotions. This type of sale is the wrong way of selling the products and services and would not be successful in long term. Strangely, lot of sales-persons relies on push sales concept for selling their products.

The other type of sales is pull sales. In this concept the sales-person would convince the potential buyer about the product and service which she is selling, considering the needs and demands of the potential buyer. The buyer would show the interest in the offerings of the sales-person and after a satisfactory discussion the sale would be closed, generally initiated by the buyer. Pull sales would satisfy everyone involved in the process and a long term relationship would start between buyer and the seller.

The concept of push sales is effective in few instances where the potential buyer is confused and buys the product in confusion. The buyer may regret his decision of buying the product afterwards; this cannot be a long term strategy in selling. Push sales concept generally work for commodities which have no differentiation, similar quality and negligible difference in prices. You may see the real life cases in push sales at roadside markets and tourist spots.

One of the main purposes of marketing team is to indirectly invigorate pull for the company's products and services through advertising and promotional events. Pull sales strategy requires a lot of resources and efforts, but this is the only strategy which can work for long term. The cost-benefit-analysis of the pull and push sales would clarify the strength of pull sales concept. A high value product or a latest technology product can only be sold through pull sales strategy. A push sales concept in these cases would work against the sales-person and the company. A technology product like smartphone is sold through pull sales strategy as the potential buyer is attracted to the product through advertisements and promotions and wants to experience the product in the showroom, before taking the final decision.

You need to plan a pull sales strategy for your products and services. You need to work with your marketing team to devise strategies to excite and inform the prospects about your products and services. During sales presentation the case for your products and services should be strong enough to convince prospect through logical and emotional reasoning to buy from your company.

## Sales Mantra 39 – Get Buy-ins

This is the logical step in the decision making process as others opinions broadens the view of the decision maker and the probability of the correctness of the action rises. In case of a family buying a product the main decision maker would be the adults of the family, especially the female adult. Generally, she would take the opinion of the other members of the family like her husband and kids to finalize her decision to buy the product. When a sales-person sells the concept, product or service to these opinion makers then it is considered as buy-ins. These buy-ins would help you by getting the advocates of your product in the prospect's team, which would improve your probability of selling the product with the affirmative decision of the decision maker.

Buy-ins are a very important factor in selling as it involves influencing the opinion makers. These opinion makers can be the experts in their own field and their opinion is sought by decision maker at the time of finalizing the sales deal. For example, the decision of buying a manufacturing machine would be taken by the top management, but the opinion makers may include the technology manager, operations manager, supervisors and even workers who would operate the machine. In this case you need to sell this product separately to each of these opinion makers as even a single objection can obstruct the close of sale. Business consultants are the master of buy-ins. These consultants convince every important manager and executive in the organization about their recommendations, much before the submission of their report to the management. During the final presentations they get the appreciation from the all concerned teams as they were already sold on the recommendations.

The sales team needs to research the prospect's company for the details of the opinion makers and influencers. You need to meet them separately and sell the concept to them before the main sales meeting with the decision makers. During these buy-ins discussions you would also encounter the objections which could be raised during the final meeting, for which you can prepare well with robust answers.

## Sales Mantra 40 – Love for Travel

Generally, all sales jobs require travelling. It is required to meet the prospects and customers to present their products and to take feedback. You also need to travel to explore the markets and build the business network for getting leads and references for filling the sales funnel. Travelling helps a sales-person by building relationships which would be used for closing the sales. The sales-person should love travelling to become a master in the domain.

Sales-person having difficulty in travelling would try to avoid it, even for important meetings. These people would like to do sales only using phone and internet. They would find various reasons to avoid travelling and even influence other team members negatively. This is bad for business. They either need to learn to like travelling or they should change their domain of work to a more 'in-office' job.

Each traveling should lead to add substantial value to the sales process. Manager and sales team needs to know the real objective of the meeting (which requires travelling), its importance and priority. The event needs to be evaluated properly and decision for travelling needs to be taken based upon the value addition through travelling. It is important to note that the love for travelling should not lead to travelling for no proper reason.

The sales manager needs to hire those sales-persons who have no issues with travelling and should be ready for out-office jobs. Existing sales-persons who have problems with travelling can be shifted to in-office jobs like sales co-ordination or pre-sales.

## Sales Mantra 41 – Dressing and Grooming

Ask any sales-person about a successful meeting and the reasons for its impact; most of the time she would talk about the great first impression. This initial impression is important in a way that it becomes the reference point for the whole meeting. A bad first impression would pull the effectiveness of the meeting down, while an initial positive impact in the sales meeting would give the 'benefit of doubt' to the sales-person for her mistakes. In fact, a fine connect with the prospect in the beginning of the meeting would support the sales-person in convincing the prospect about the quality and the value proposition of the product.

For creating a good first impression the most important aspects are the physical attributes of the sales-person, which means the way you dress and prepare yourself for the client meetings. A shoddily dressed sales-person would leave a bad impression on the customers while a well-dressed and groomed person would bring positivity to the meeting room, while presenting herself as a sincere person. In addition to dressing you need to confidently carry yourself, as if you are doing a great job by selling your products. Your body language also communicates the non-verbal messages to the customers.

Most of the time formal dressing is preferred for sales meeting but in recent times the technology entrepreneurs have changed the trend by dressing casually, even for important meeting and presentations. The logical way for sales meeting is to match the dressing of your prospect. The purpose of dressing is to create a pleasant impression on the prospect. The dressing and grooming has no role in selling except creating the initial image about the sales-person, but as discussed before it is important and has its reasons.

The dressing depends upon the type of your prospect. The prospect could be a technology startup where everyone is dressed casually. A person in complete formals would look a bit out of place at these meetings. Similarly, a banking client would appreciate formals instead of casuals.

The best suggestion for the sales-person would be dress herself in the cloths in which she is comfortable. She needs to be well groomed, comfortable and should know to confidently carry herself. In fact, formal clothing would be appreciated in any formal meeting.

The sales manager needs to decide upon the clothing for the sales team. This depends upon the customer segment and the company's policies about dressing for work. It is also important to choose the comfortable clothing for your sales team.

## Sales Mantra 42 – Perseverance

For every sales-person a successful sales meeting with the prospect is experienced only after a series of unsuccessful meetings. As this is a general fact of the job of sales, the sales-person needs to be strong physically and emotionally to face the challenges and pressures of unsuccessful meetings. The master key for the strength required for these sales meetings is patience, and it would be required every day for most of the meetings.

Sometimes, you may encounter a case where a seemingly easy deal may take forever to close or an adorable customer becomes a most fierce critic of your products and services or even you. Sometimes, a sales deal at the verge of closing would be delayed by the decision maker by citing meaningless reasons. This list may go on. The point which you need to understand is that the patience is the key for closing the sales.

Another closely linked concept with sales is perseverance. This means that you have enough physical and mental strength and determination to persist for the sales deal, to close and to achieve the sales target. Perseverance requires determination for sales and persistence for the deal. Most of the time your sales deals would be delayed or kept hanging for some reason or the other, and as you cannot force the prospect to close it, you need to persevere. You need to use your skills to put an endurable pressure on the decision maker to take the decision. The sales-person who is able to manage these forces would become a successful sales-person.

Patience and perseverance are two important abilities which are not only helpful in sales but in your personal life too.

Now the complex question is how to search for the excellent sales-persons with abilities of patience and perseverance? It takes a lot of time to develop these abilities in people who have low level of patience and perseverance. These two abilities are considered as the basic nature of an individual and it requires a lot of determination and commitment to develop even a part of these capabilities. What should a sales manager do to make her sales team behave with patience and perseverance?

The manager needs to set strict rules for expected behaviors during the sales process. She needs to specify various scenarios in sales process and expected behavior and actions by the sales-person. The manager must be extremely strict for the execution of these rules, which would force the sales team to behave and act in the right way during certain complex circumstances of sales process. For example, if a sales deal is delayed then the expected action would be to remain calm and composed and to keep a light pressure on the decision maker to close the deal. The sales-person is not allowed to get irritated or get into conflict of any type, due to delay in decisions by prospect.

With time these rules would become the culture of the company making sales team to behave in the right way during the sales process.

## Sales Mantra 43 – Know When to Move Out

A master sales-person knows when to move out. Many times, for cracking a sales deal, you may interact with wrong person who is not a decision maker; you need to politely move away from him as he would not add any value, instead would waste your time and suck your energy. Sometimes, you are meeting with the right person, who is the decision maker, but in-spite of all your efforts the sale in not closing. The reasons could vary from budget problems to intensity of requirement. Whatever the reason, you need to decide a final point to close the sales deal, after which you need to politely move out after thanking the customer for his time.

This is an essential judgment which every sales-person needs to make, many times in their business meetings. Any wrong judgment may lead to lost sale and spoiled relationship, for which you need to be careful about. You need to perform an extensive research about the prospect's company to get the grasp about the major issues of their company. The more informed you are, the better would be your judgments, decisions and actions.

You need to develop the skills of politely ending a sales discussion and moving out, without feeling offended or making them feel guilty. These skills would be extremely beneficial in life too.

## Sales Mantra 44 – Intrapreneurship

An entrepreneur is a risk taker who identifies an opportunity in the market and develops and delivers required product or service to the market. The entrepreneur is passionate and enthusiastic about work and remains optimistic about success. An intrapreneur is an entrepreneur inside an organization. Though she is an employee of the organization but she thinks and acts like an entrepreneur. She is completely sincere about the success of her organization and performs at her peak to ensure this success. She knows the concept of self-motivation, which helps her to face hardships and complexities of her job. She has synchronized her personal goals with the organizational goals and her energy is completely focused on winning.

As an entrepreneur, she has the complete confidence in her abilities and is always ready to take risks. She enjoys her work and is highly efficient and productive in her tasks. This attitude makes her an important employee of her organization and management cares for her success and satisfaction.

On a general note, not only sales-person but every employee of the company should try to be an intrapreneur.

An intrapreneur in sales team would be an asset for the company. She would be a hardworking person and the most efficient team member. Her sales presentations are always excellent and her relationship with customers is great. They care for her as she cares for them. She is empathetic about the needs of the customers and works with various teams of the organization to deliver value to customers. She is passionate about her work and is completely honest to it. She looks happy and satisfied with her job.

To be an intrapreneur, you need to have a slight change in mindset. You need to have big goals in life; your ambitions can help you to decide on those goals. In fact, many people have goals in their lives but do not act on it, due to trivial reasons. It is important to understand that to achieve life goals; a person needs to take action for it. You need to develop required skills, take logical risks and work hard. To become a person who would achieve these goals, you will first need to become an intrapreneur, which would be your first step to achieve that goal. If you excel in intrapreneurship, then you are entitled to move forward towards your goals.

## Sales Mantra 45 – More Value to Customers

A master sales-person understands the true meaning of value. She understands the value of relationship between her and the organization she serves. She also understands the activities & tasks in sales cycle and the value delivered by each. She has the complete knowledge of the value proposition of her organizations products and services and the various ways the value would be delivered to the customers. She also knows about the actions which damages value.

Her understanding of value is deep enough to get clarity about business relations, which are based upon mutual value addition. She knows the similar relation exist between her and her customers. That is the reason she is extremely sincere about value addition to her customers. She knows that the products and services sold by her to customers must deliver the promised value, to build the relationship stronger. She takes extra efforts to ensure that the promised value is received by the customers. Her concern about value addition makes her unique as a master sales-person and these efforts make her the trusted partner of her customers who would take extra efforts to make her successful.

You need to understand the concept of value in your job and your work. Your relation with your customer is the value addition equivalent to the amount of money paid by customer. Generally, it is the promise which you make for your products and services. You just need to make sure that promise is delivered. This is the key to customer's satisfaction. To delight your customers, you need to give extra value in addition to the promised value.

Same rule can be applied with respect to your relation with your organization, which assigns you certain responsibilities. If you could deliver more value to your company, then you become the star of your company.

## Sales Mantra 46 – Learner

A great sales-person is an excellent learner. She learns from her fellow team members, seniors, gurus and books. She is an expert in the products and services she sells and is updated about any new additions to them. Most of the time she does not require pre-sales or technical people for their support in presentation, as she can handle most of the prospect's questions, herself.

She even learns from the sales experts from other industries and markets and implements relevant techniques for her cause. She constantly works with other departments like marketing, pre-sales, technology and operation to look for new ideas and knowledge. She reads a lot, attends seminars and workshops for improving her skills and competencies. She likes her job and wants to be best in it.

You need to build a learning culture in your team. Your team needs to regularly discuss the successful experiences and resolutions of problems to learn from each other. You can arrange for discussions of new ideas from experts and master sales-persons. This learning culture would bring the team together and make them enthusiastic about the job.

## Sales Mantra 47 – Feedback

Feedback is the process of interacting with your customers to understand their experiences with the products and services sold to them during the selling cycle. These feedbacks are tough to take as an unsatisfied customer may demand his money back and can create all sorts of hassles. But, these feedbacks, if taken and used properly, can take your to the next level. Both of following aspects are important:

- Receiving the feedback from customers and
- Acting on those feedback

A company would be successful only if its customers are satisfied with the products and services supplied to them. If in any case the customers are not satisfied then it is important for the company to know about it and rectify it. Company with unsatisfied customers cannot survive for long. Generally, marketing team takes the responsibility to analyze the experience of the customers with the company's products, which is an organized and formal process. It would be better if every sales-person also takes the feedback of her customers. Most of the time the problems are minor and can be resolved immediately; these solutions must not be delayed for a later time. The feedback process of sales team would also connect them better with customers, who can help in increasing sales by references, leads and repeat sales.

You should design a feedback process for yourself and your team. Feedback should be taken at certain intervals after closing the sale, when the product is delivered and it is being used by the customer. Service feedback can be taken immediately, for example, many restaurants and hotels ask for the feedback after services are delivered.

## Sales Mantra 48 – Objections

A successful sales-person is the master in handling objections. The objections are the logical or illogical reasons given by the prospect for delaying the closing of sales. The objections of the prospect may look something like:

- We do not have the budget
- Your prices are too high
- Your product do not have all the features
- We will get back to you
- We are getting better deals from other companies
- I need to discuss it with my team
- Top management is not interested now
- The decision is postponed by few months

Sometimes, they may come with unique and strange objections to delay their decisions.

Every sales-person faces the objection like these and they act like the biggest obstruction in meeting their sales targets. Most of the sale persons are afraid of the objections raised by the prospects. The successful sales-person embraces the objection and uses it to build the case for their products and services. She would use their objections to build pressure on them for closing the sale. She is aware about the client's situation and has enough information to support them in decision making. She does her homework on objections in detail and has the ready impactful answers for each of those objections, leading to closing the sale. She would prepare and collect the supporting documents and information to make her case stronger. In addition to these efforts, she would get the buy-ins from the prospects team to put more pressure on the decision maker.

You need to prepare a complete list of objections raised by your prospects and customers. You should work with your team and seniors executives to get guidance in directing these objections to neutral state, even using these objections to close your sale. You need to work for the best answers with supporting material to prove your point.

## Sales Mantra 49 – Receive Payments

Most of the time it is the responsibility of the sales-person to collect money from the client for the sale of products. This is important as the sales would be considered complete only after the payments for the sale of product is transferred to your company's account. Sometimes, the customer creates resistance to release payments and delays it consistently. The behavior of these customers wastes your time and affects your company revenues and cash flow. Therefore, it is important to have the clear payment schedule even before closing the sales. It is important that the customer agrees on this schedule in non-verbal format, which means that either it is on paper or agreed through e-mail.

You need to be clear and firm about your agreed payment schedule. To achieve that you may request, pressurize or argues with the customer for the release of payment. It would be great if you can understand the payment behavior of the client, so that you can plan in advance about receiving your payments from the customer.

A good sales-person would know the ways to get her payment released from the customer. You need to know the right persons to meet and hot buttons to press. Your initial prospect analysis would help you with this case.

You need to check all of the organization's prospects and customers for their payment history. You also need to identify the ways to get money in shortest possible time from your customers, without any hassles.

## Sales Mantra 50 – Repeat Sales

For a successful sales-person one of the biggest source of getting the business is the pool of existing customers. She builds a long term relationship with her customers and keeps interacting with them through greetings and information sharing. She keeps serving them through her after-sales-support team which ensures the satisfactory experience of customers. She occasionally visits them for asking for business in disguise of meeting them to ensure satisfaction from their products and services.

If a sales-person is able to build deep relationship with customers by using various skills and competencies then she would be at the top of the mind for every customer. This connection would make her customers call her for any requirement of her company's products and services. As you are able to sell again to your customers this is called repeat sales. Repeat sale is important as it happens only when the customer is completely satisfied with your products, services and support. He is happy with the sales-person and wants to connect with her again for any new requirements. These customers also become advocates for your company's products and services in the market.

You need to take special care for your existing customers as they are easiest to sell. If you are able to maintain these relations well then your major chunk of business would come from existing customers. They would also provide you leads and references for selling your products and services.

Check your present repeat sales percentage in total sales. If your percentage is not high then you need to find the reasons for missing this opportunity. Develop a plan to connect with them and take required actions to get repeat business from them. You can take the support of the marketing team to design various promotional packages for the existing customers. Your purpose should be to improve the percentage of repeat business in your total sales.

## Sales Mantra 51 – Self-Branding

In many cases the customer buys from the sales-person instead of the company, which means that the brand of the sales-person is more important than the brand of the company. This sales-person act as the advisor to the customer who rely on the suggestions of the sales-person for buying the products, services or solutions. This sales-person has built such a good rapport and strong relationship that the customer trusts her.

This type of branding takes time and effort on the part of sales-person. Sales-person needs to build knowledge base for being an expert in the domain, who is able to help customers with her knowledge for taking decisions. She needs to have a strong network in the market for solving product related issues for the buyer. She needs to be popular by being an active member in industry by giving lectures and keynotes. Also, she needs to involve herself in other activities which would lead to building her brand image.

This brand image needs to be positive, you would not like to have a brand image of a sales-person who is too pushy or who do not keep her commitment. It is necessary that your brand image is positive which supports you in your sales. This brand image is essential in getting the meetings with the decision makers and in building instant rapport with customers. Brand image of the sales-person would support her in getting the required trust for closing the sales and getting repeat business.

You, as a sales-person should build your independent brand image in the market. You can associate yourself with several industry and sales associations where you can be an active person who is adding value to its members. You can take initiations to be a speaker at conferences and seminars where you can share your experiences and views. These efforts would improve your credibility and make you trustworthy in market and in the eyes of the prospects and customers.

# About Author

Anshuman is an entrepreneur and investor and has been instrumental in nurturing many successful companies. He has created of several successful companies in various domains. He is also involved in supporting development of several other companies. In business, his interests lie in cutting edge technologies and innovative services.

His guidance has helped many businessman, investors and entrepreneurs to succeed in their businesses. He has also supported several entrepreneurship cells and incubation centers.

He is an engineer and a management graduate. He can be reached at anshuman.connect@gmail.com

www.ingramcontent.com/pod-product-compliance
Lightning Source LLC
Chambersburg PA
CBHW071525180526
45171CB00002B/379